BRITAIN IN OLD PHOTOGRAPHS

WOKINGHAM

B O B   W Y A T T

ALAN SUTTON PUBLISHING LIMITED

Alan Sutton Publishing Limited
Phoenix Mill · Far Thrupp · Stroud
Gloucestershire · GL5 2BU

First published 1995

Cover photographs: (front) Caiger's shoe shop at 13 Peach Street; (back) a carnival parade, 1920s.

British Library Cataloguing in Publication Data.
A catalogue record for this book is available from
the British Library.

ISBN 0-7509-0980-3

Typeset in 9/10 Sabon.
Typesetting and origination by
Alan Sutton Publishing Limited.
Printed in Great Britain by
Ebenezer Baylis, Worcester.

Langborough Recreation ground, for many years a public open space, from the path leading from Gipsy Lane. This photograph shows the lime trees in their infancy in the early years of this century. Another row of trees has since been planted beside them to take over when they die.

Contents

The street layout of Wokingham based upon the 1853 Tithe map, showing the basic street pattern which has survived throughout the history of the town. Opposite is an aerial view taken in the 1930s, which shows All Saints' church before the Norreys estate was built. Note the original position of Cross Street.

Introduction

There has been a settlement on the site of Wokingham since Saxon times. Called previously Ockingham or Oakingham, it seems possible that the territory was inhabited by the Wockingas who lived in what was then little more than a clearing in the Royal forest. A building for Christian worship has been on the site of the present All Saints' church since Saxon times and the residents of the little town – no more than a few hundred by then – tilled the land, wove silk and cloth and exercised the various crafts necessary to sustain the town and those who lived in the surrounding countryside. There were wheelwrights, blacksmiths, shopkeepers, butchers, bakers, brewers and publicans, sometimes in seemingly greater quantities than appeared sustainable. They all contributed to the success of the close-knit community, with surrounding estates and farms providing most of the employment.

Although the boundaries of the town have been extended greatly over the last few decades, the town centre street layout has not changed very much from the earliest times. The direction of the traffic and its volume has altered, and the one-way system now starts at Peach Street. Many of the buildings have been modified considerably, but London Road still passes All Saints' church on the right. At the fine town hall the road branches left to Denmark Street, right to Broad Street and thence to Reading. Leading off from the Market Place, Rose Street, which contains some of the oldest buildings in the town, goes off to the right, and at the end of Broad Street Milton Road leads to Twyford and Henley.

Now surrounded by new estates, fighting to keep sacrosanct its small remaining green gaps to prevent it from becoming part of an unidentified urban sprawl, and at the same time conscious of the changes in shopping patterns, Wokingham strives to stay a living town with an active centre, catering for the needs of high tech industries and commerce, and yet to preserve its essential character.

The population of the parish of Wokingham, which then included much of the surrounding countryside, had reached only 3,254 by 1891; by 1901 there were a few more people at 3,551. By 1911, when many of the photographs in this book were taken, the figure had risen to 4,352. Numbers rose more rapidly as time went on. This small, compact market town has a fascinating history, a history contained in documents and records and in old newspapers. It has, too, spoken memories and – over the last 100 years or so – many visual memorials in old photographs. The small selection contained in this book gives a flavour of what the town looked like, what its people did, and shows what has changed and what has been preserved.

A sketch of the earlier Guildhall on the present Town Hall site.

Section One

THE TOWN HALL

The original timber building was built some time between 1612 and 1625. It was taken

down in 1858, and the present beautiful building was constructed on the site by public

subscription at the cost of £3,500, £2,000 being subscribed by the County Police

Committee so that the county police station could be included. The picture shows a busy

cattle market day at the turn of the century.

The Town Hall was opened by the Lord High Steward, Lord Braybrooke, on 6 June 1860. This is the earliest known photograph of the building, possibly taken within a few years of the opening. The large tree might be the one shown in the drawing of the original Guildhall (see page 6).

Traffic had increased by the 1940s, a bus stop with shelter has appeared and cars park in the Market Place.

John Headington, the owner of the brewery and several public houses in the town, had been a councillor since 1890 and was Borough Mayor in 1903/4. This picture, the only one known of the interior of the Town Hall from that period, shows the table set out for the Mayoral banquet on 9 November 1903. There were sixty-four guests and the total cost was £94. The picture is interesting as it shows the original positions of the portraits and the dark staining of the woodwork, which has since been stripped.

Bullnose Morris and horse-drawn milk float, 1920s.

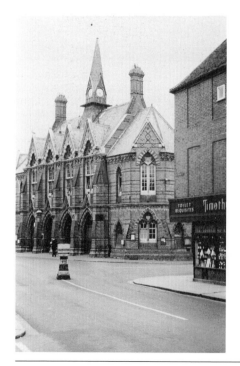

This end of the building shows the fire station. On the right is Timothy Whites, one of the town's chemists until it joined up with Boots, which is now just out of the picture to the left.

THE TOWN

Looking down Peach Street from the Market Place, c. 1900. It is likely that the road was being dug up to lay the main sewer. Most of these buildings have now gone.

Another view looking down Peach Street, taken from almost the same place as the one on the previous page, but some years earlier.

A sunny day with all the blinds out, but very little activity apart from the odd cyclist. The gasworks were built in 1849 and one of the gas lamp standards is shown.

The photographer of this picture must have stood just in front of the gas lamp. It is quite a busy day, with two-way traffic and a lorry unloading.

At the Overhangs in Peach Street when the almshouses still stood, and before the Victorian buildings on the left were replaced by the unsightly concrete shops.

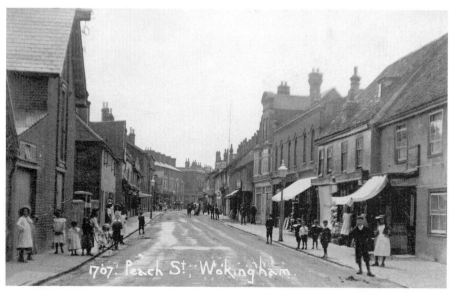

Looking up Peach Street towards the Town Hall, *c*. 1910.

This is a particularly interesting view taken in 1949. On the right and at the corner stands the old gas lamp, with the newly erected sodium electric light standard next to it.

On entering the town from Bracknell, opposite All Saints' church, stood the almshouses, first endowed by Thomas Westende in 1451 and rebuilt in 1830, and Queen Victoria House – two cottages built in 1887. Walking by are Mr and Mrs Whittingham, who lived in London Road. He was a bell-ringer at the church. Members of the Caiger family, who owned the electrical shop on the right, still live in Wokingham.

A very early picture of Broad Street, with very little going on. The road was constructed of stones and always had a covering of dust in the summer and mud in the winter; the pathway in the foreground helped pedestrians on wet days. Note the narrow entrance to Rose Street on the right.

Broad Street, before 1912. The cross marks the old post office, close to where the present one stands. Of particular interest is the ramshackle building third from the left, used as a junk shop, next to the one with the upper bay windows and the curved top. The latter is used by a building society today.

By the time this picture was taken the Electric Theatre – a cinema – occupies the site of the junk shop, and the building has been made to match the one next to it; it too is now a building society. Most people thought that they had been built together until these pictures came to light. A close look at the two buildings shows that there are minor differences in construction.

Looking down Broad Street towards Tudor House.

These buildings stood at the end of Broad Street as part of Perkins' Garage. They were demolished in 1963 and the wooden garage building went some time after, to be replaced by a filling station and then with the present Georgian-style office.

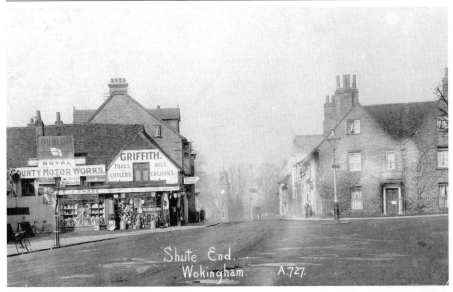

The garage is on the left, and Tudor House, the doctors' surgery, are seen here in the early years of the century when the beams were covered with plaster. Some of the beams came from Billingbear House, which burnt down and was demolished in the 1920s. At that time Tudor House was used as a private school.

No. 41 Broad Street is on the right. It still has the leafy cladding, but the iron railings went for scrap metal during the last war. Tudor House looks much as it does now. The trees died and an ugly series of traffic lights have added little to the scene.

An early view of Shute End. Much of the scene remains, despite today's traffic. St Paul's parish rooms, which include a clock tower, were built in 1893 by the Walter family. These are still in use, although now for different purposes.

Again, little has changed. A mini-roundabout fills the road in front of The Terrace.

Looking up Denmark Street from Langborough Road corner. On the left can be seen part of the Primitive Methodist church, where the Job Centre now stands.

Pictures of Denmark Street are hard to find. This one looks up towards the Town Hall and dates from the 1920s. Tesco's entrance now stands on the left, but the drill hall cottages are still there, now used as shops. These stood in front of the Drill Hall and were occupied by the caretaker and the drill sergeant. On the right is the Royal Exchange pub – no longer there.

Walker's grocery store in the Market Place, now gone.

A view taken from the roof of the Town Hall overlooking the Red Lion, 1950s.

Again from the Town Hall roof, looking down at what is now Iceland's shop on the corner of Luckley Path.

Market Place, looking down Peach Street. Colebrook's the butcher and fishmonger is on the right and the boarded up shop is being prepared for Mrs Moore's high-class tobacconist and confectionery shop.

The Market Place, with Talbot's (formerly Jefferies') coal office on the right.

Heelas' departmental store, where Boots now stands. The small shop of theirs on the left was once Perkins' cycle shop.

The Market Place, looking from the other direction; by this time the motor car has taken over. Free parking was possible on all of the streets in the 1950s.

The line of Tudor cottages in Rose Street has now been refurbished.

Nos 13–21 Rose Street. The site is now occupied by the Waitrose car park.

Peach Street, the site of the present parade of shops.

Milton Road was the main road to Twyford and Henley. This photograph was taken looking away from the town just past the Baptist church, before the First World War.

Looking up towards the town, 1904. Martins Pool was built later just around the corner on the right.

STREETS AND PATHS

East Heath Avenue, a country lane off the Finchampstead Road, summer 1912.

Gipsy Lane, 1920s. This was an old drovers' road, and although the elm trees have now gone it still has the sunken appearance. Houses have been built on both sides, and driving and walking along it is somewhat more hazardous than it was when this picture was taken.

Looking into the town at the first of the railway bridges in Finchampstead Road. Molly Millars Lane is on the left, and the houses on the right are still there.

Luckley Lane, before the First World War. This is now Luckley Road, and further along it still stand the Lucas Almshouses.

Emmbrook Road. On the right, part of the wall of the Rifle Volunteer pub can just be seen.

The sheep wash, *c.* 1910. Most of the roads around the countryside were rough tracks when this picture was taken. One former resident states that this is now the footpath that goes to Ludgrove across the railway footbridge in Gipsy Lane, that the wood in the background was known as Bigwood, and that Chapel Green is on the right. All this is unlikely to be the case.

It is not possible to see the convent in Easthampstead Road as clearly as this today. A house stands where the photographer stood and trees obscure the view.

Easthampstead Road, looking towards Peach Street. Some of the buildings are still in use, but car parks are on both sides of the road. The old Ritz cinema was built on the left.

Station Road, looking towards the station, 1915. The Roman Catholic priest lived in the house on the right. The laundry was just beyond the first telegraph pole on the right.

Reading Road, looking towards the town from the point to which the borough boundary was extended in 1927.

Murdoch Road, with Sturges Road on the right, *c.* 1925. The house on the right has been converted into four flats. It was once owned by Captain Dawes of the Royal Irish Dragoon Guards.

A very leafy Murdoch Road, 1912. Most of the Morris-designed houses would have been built in the woodlands of the Batty's Barn estate.

Most of these houses in Sturges Road are easy to identify today.

The same applies to this muddy Crescent Road, looking towards Sturges Road, 1911. Briarwood, the house at the top, cannot now be seen because of the trees which have grown in front of it.

A view down Langborough Road, looking towards the Duke's Head, *c.* 1910.

Langborough Road again, from a slightly different position, with the grocer's shop/sub-post office on the right.

A view down Reading Road, with the Rifle Volunteer on the left. The name of the pub celebrates the Berkshire Rifle Volunteers who met at the Drill Hall, and no doubt at this pub!

Section Four

SHOPS AND
BUSINESSES

Caiger's shoe shop at 13 Peach Street, is now a building society and is next door to the electricity showrooms. Mr Caiger stands at the door with a soldier at the end of the First World War. The notice above the shop welcomes the boys home.

By now, the Heelas empire had extended its building to the edge of Rose Street. The most attractive Victorian building at the corner is sadly missed.

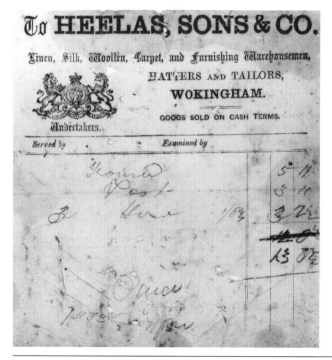

A typical mid-nineteenth century receipt from Heelas. Someone took the trouble to frame it at the time.

The old Colebrook's store in the Market Place, on the corner of Luckley Path, became David Greig's. It is now altered considerably on the ground floor, and houses the Iceland shop.

Any excuse was made to decorate a shop – which one is this?

Stevens' basket shop, Broad Street, *c.* 1900. This building, next to the post office, is another one that has survived. Stevens' had been in business since 1785; they had a factory at Crondall, and shops in Bracknell, Farnham and this one in Wokingham, which was opened in 1859. They sold cots, brushes, wheelchairs, baskets and childrens' hoops, which can be seen on the right of the picture. Above is a notice for Giles the signwriter of London Road, and above was a photographic studio, which accounts for the fact that the two upper windows are covered up.

Clark's grocery shop is now Carpenters, in Denmark Street. It was in the basement here that the town's first newspaper, *The Wokingham and Bracknell Gazette*, was born on 24 January 1903. It is now the *Wokingham Times*.

Sidney Pither in the doorway of his butcher's shop in Broad Street, during the First World War. On the brickwork of the tall wall at the side, his name and the fact that he was a purveyor of high class meat can still be seen.

Mr Evans the harness maker sold riding equipment from his shop at 19 Peach Street (now Toy World). Mr Rideout, who stands on the right of the picture, was killed in the First World War. The photograph dates from about 1912.

This was Brant's butcher's shop in Broad Street, *c*. 1912. At one time there were eight butchers in the town. This later became Perkins' garage.

Mr Stevens outside his hairdresser's shop at 6 Oxford Road, 1920s.

This fine old photograph shows Mr Jefferies, the coal merchant, ouside his shop in the Market Place. If the passer-by looks up above Super Snaps, the black semicircle that once contained the white letters 'Coal Office' can still be seen.

Mr Merritt with his horse Billy, who carried coal to many Wokingham houses, 1927.

Mr Jefferies' cart, with a large lump of coal that had just been unloaded from a railway wagon. A raffle was held to guess its weight – tickets cost 6d. each.

The Andrews family ran this large laundry in Station Road until the 1950s.

The washing machines of the day, 1930s.

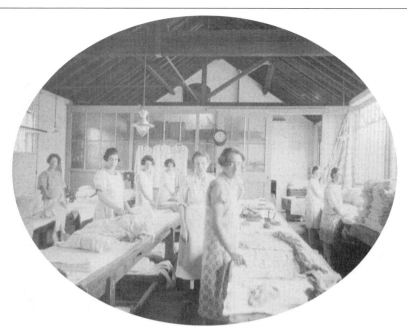

Many of the ladies of the town ironed and folded the clean clothes.

Goswell's, the tailor in the Market Place.

Headington's brewery, 1890s. It stood on the site which is now partly occupied by Tesco's.

Section Five

TRANSPORT

Wokingham station. The railway had come to the town in 1849.

Strawberry ices ready for the peace celebrations, 1919.

An unknown carriage outside the Wheatsheaf in the Market Place, 1901.

In 1909, in a shed said to have been located on the corner of Goodchild Road and Easthampstead Road (where the ambulance station is today), Mr Fairbrother, a journeyman carpenter, made this flying machine, which despite its appearance was not an airship. A number of local people subscribed to what was known as the Wokingham Whale. It was taken to Windsor for an engine to be installed, but nothing more was heard of it. Mr Fairbrother also built a flimsy aeroplane, which is supposed to have flown a foot from the ground!

A nice view of the station and the railway buildings – all very Victorian.

The level-crossing is still there to hold up the traffic. This picture, dating from about 1920, looks towards the town with Oxford Road on the left, before the signal-box was built. The gates were opened mechanically by turning a large wheel in the box. At the time that this picture was taken, the gate was manually operated from the ground.

The station, 1916. This pleasant little Victorian building was replaced for no good reason by an inadequate and unattractive building, soon itself to be replaced.

A splendid view of the railway station, *c.* 1910. This shows the footbridge, which is still in use.

It took all of these men – and the horse – to operate the station. The photograph dates from about 1912.

The station staff, and horses. The animal on the right was used for shunting, and is being held by Mr Marshall.

The shunting horse doing his work.

MOTOR REMOVALS & HAULAGE CONTRACTORS.

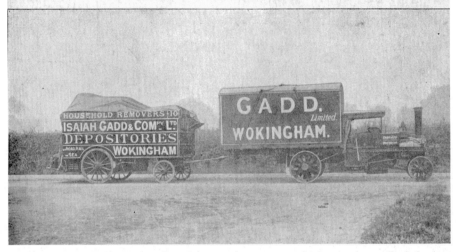

Isaiah Gadd had this and at least three other steam vehicles at the end of the last century. He had a removal business, a furniture shop and was a coal merchant.

A big job for his successor – seven container loads on railway trucks at the sidings of Wokingham station.

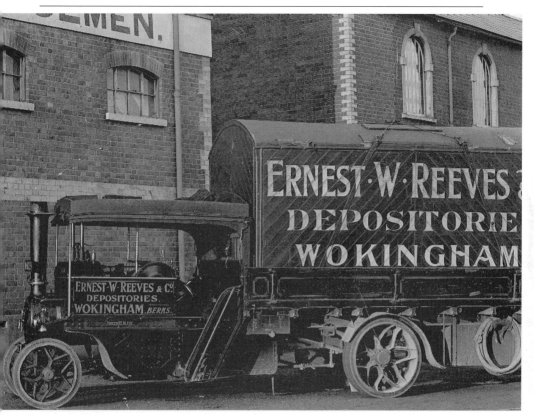

Ernest Reeves was a clerk with Heelas in Reading and he came to the town to manage Gadd's removal business as a young man in his early twenties, in about 1911. When Gadd died, Jefferies took over the coal side, Welch the furniture and Reeves, in partnership with Vale, took over the removal business. Just after the First World War, steam took over from the horse; a resident remembers that in 1914 it took three-and-a-half days to carry his furniture from London to Wokingham by horse-drawn vehicle. The premises were on the corner of Finchampstead Road and Carey Road. Later on another depository was built in Carey Road. They have both gone.

In the early 1920s the petrol lorry slowly replaced steam; this one had solid rubber tyres.

A Dennis of the mid-1930s.

By now the business had expanded and there were nine vehicles. Reeves was one of the first removal firms in the area to use the new-fangled pneumatic tyres. The trailer at the back still has solids, and was the one that used to be towed by the steam vehicle.

The same container on a new chassis, No. 27, could also draw a trailer. It was bought in the 1940s, by which time the firm was also established in Camberley.

The ultimate removal van, *c.* 1948. Reeves used this body built by Alan Perkins at his works in Reading – the Wokingham Pantechnicon. It had a maximum legal speed of 30 m.p.h., and is seen here being driven by Bill Tanner.

The Headington family had one of the first cars in Wokingham. This is their Darracq of about 1904.

A float lined up in Rectory Road for the peace celebrations, 1919. By this time the car population in Wokingham had risen beyond the half dozen or so in the early years of motoring.

Even more cars, late 1920s. Now there was a garage that specialised in selling them as well as for repairs. This is Perkins' garage at the end of Broad Street with a selection of Morris cars.

Another peace celebrations picture from 1919. Unlike Mr Fairbrother's machine, this airship was not even meant to fly.

Section Six

PEOPLE AND EVENTS

The chefs get ready for Queen Victoria's Diamond Jubilee celebrations, 1897.

By donkey, trap, bicycle and on foot – almost the entire town came to the ox-roasting outside the Town Hall in 1897. The Wokingham Town Silver Band was there.

Partaking in the Coronation Dinner in the Market Place, 26 June 1902.

Miss Gadd, daughter of Isaiah and a Wesleyan Methodist (the letters IG can be seen on the façade of a house he built opposite the Methodist Church in Rose Street) formed this mandoline band in about 1910.

She was also a leading light in the Wesleyan Orchestra. Mr Ayres is on the base, Charlie Blake is one of the violinists, and Miss Gadd sits in gown and mortarboard.

Cole's confectioner and tobacconist shop stood at the corner of Easthampstead Road and Peach Street. He took it over from Miss Blea and Miss Hazel in the 1920s, and the Cole family lived above the shop until it was sold to Mr Hawkins in the 1930s. Mr Cole closed up the doorway and placed another window on the Peach Street frontage, also building a corner entrance. Mr Hocking was the next owner, and then it went to Mrs Plumridge until it was closed in the 1950s. It is now Lucan's Bistro. The little girl in the doorway is Mary Cole, who became the supervisor of the town telephone exchange. The picture on the right shows the complex manual exchange with some of its thirty operators on the last day of its operation in 1975. It was housed above the present Broad Street post office. Among the operators shown are Janice Fletcher, May Eccles, Daphne Geldsetzer, Denis Walker and Mary Cole, who still lives only a few streets away from the family's old shop.

The Guide Lieutenant, Miss Joyce Smith, at her marriage to Edmund Lee at the Methodist church in Rose Street, 1948. Many of these girls still live in the town.

Sarah Jane Harris (née Cheeseman) cousin of Alderman Cheeseman, mayor in 1943/4, photographed in 1885 at the age of sixteen. The photographer was H.E. Hall of Ducie Lodge, Wokingham.

Mrs Charlotte Cheeseman outside 80 Rose Street, 1930s.

Five men who went on a great nine-day caravan trip, 1911. They are Messrs Bowyer, the two Martins, Caiger and Medcalf.

James Cheeseman, the father of Alderman Cheeseman, outside the clock- and watch-makers in Barkham Road near the level crossing. He worked for Sale and Sons and died in 1927 at the age of eighty-two.

All of the employees of the Borough Council at the retirement of C.W. Marks, the borough surveyor, early 1930s.

David Goddard, the mayor in 1945/6, wearing the fine chain and badge that date from 1885.

This was the last occasion on which an ox was roasted in the Market Place – 1953.

The mayor, corporation and honorary officers, between the wars. The same style of robing – possibly even some of the same garments – is still used by the present Town Council on ceremonial occasions.

The first lady mayor, the Hon. Mrs Corfield, with her daughter, Alderman Perkins and the Catholic priest, October 1948. She held the post from 1947 to 1950.

On the left, with the wig (still worn by the present town clerk) is the then clerk J. Elliston Clifton, with the mayor, Alderman W.T. Martin, the Duke of Connaught and Mr Jefferies, the coal merchant and the man in charge of Wokingham Scouts. The Duke was in the town to take over the post of high steward.

The unveiling of the war memorial at All Saints' church, 1921.

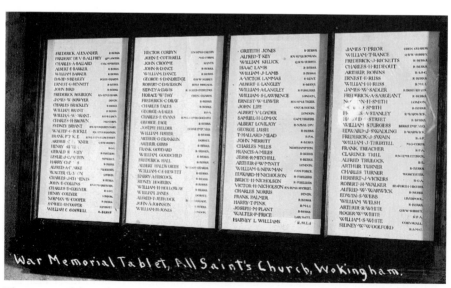

The names of those from the parish who did not return from the First World War. The main memorial, which includes soldiers from the whole borough, is in the Town Hall.

A decorated float for the peace celebrations, standing in Rectory Road, 18 October 1919. The brick wall is still a feature of the road opposite the police station.

The ox-roasting, 1911. The mayor was H.C. Mylne. Throughout the previous night the ox had been roasted by the fire brigade. The old folk were given a dinner in the Town Hall and 1,100 children gathered in the Market Place to be given Coronation medals – the fête took place in a field in Easthampstead Road. There was a carnival procession and a Bohemian Concert in the Market Place until nearly midnight.

Looking down Broad Street during the peace celebrations, 1919.

A huge crowd gathered in the Market Place.

All of the youths associated with the Methodist church joined the Boys' Brigade. It was the most popular youth movement until the Boy Scouts were formed. The lads drilled with rifles and wore a simple uniform of belt, pouch and cap. They are pictured in about 1910.

Alderman Albert Priest, a builder, leading the Corporation as mayor – he held the post from 1929 to 1933.

A huge crowd gathered for the proclamation of the accession of King George V.

The Coronation, Wokingham.
Boiling the potatoes & puddings.

Many pictures were taken of the Coronation celebrations in 1911. Here, the fire brigade is engaged in its favourite pastime – when not extinguishing fires – of boiling potatoes and puddings; the customary ox was being roasted under the awning in the background.

A jolly scene when the Council bumped the aldermen to mark the new bounds when the borough was extended in 1927. W.T. Martin is on the right.

More people at the peace celebrations, 1919.

The group of ladies outside the coal office are looking at the news bulletins pinned up there during the General Strike of 1926. Even the newspaper workers stopped work, but the government produced special news sheets.

Many sports were played in the town when this picture of the hockey team was taken in the 1920s. As well as hockey, there were two football clubs (Wokingham in Finchampstead Road and the Wokingham Old Boys on Langborough Recreation Ground), a lawn tennis and croquet club, and four cricket clubs.

Even the ladies had a cricket team; this was formed for the groundsman's benefit event in September 1910.

The ladies were much more likely to be seen in this role – serving the food! The photograph shows the gymkhana, before the First World War.

A fancy dress party for the gymkhana.

Every event had to have its officials, and they had to pose for the photographer. This is the gymkhana again.

Mayor F. Barrett plants a tree in Langborough recreation ground to celebrate the king's Jubilee in 1935.

Frank Perkins, the mayor in 1937, inspecting the town's voluntary organizations.

The very popular Wokingham character, Stanley Bowyer, owned the pet shop in Peach Street. He joined the Council in 1931 and died while still serving in the late 1980s.

Yet another proclamation, this time for the accession of Queen Elizabeth.

Outside the Ritz cinema, 1946. The event was the presentation of wallets to all the servicemen who returned home to Wokingham. The mayor at the time was David Goddard, and Frank Perkins is in the front row as the organiser of the event.

Volunteer ambulance workers at the end of the Second World War.

Frank Perkins leads the Home Guard through the Market Place, marching past the mayor, Walter Fullbrook, 1946.

Street parties are always popular with the children. This one was in Rose Street to celebrate the Coronation of Her Majesty in 1953.

Nothing is known about this picture, which must date from the early part of this century. It shows the fire team and the Deputy Captain Mr F. Caiger with the steam engine.

Section Seven

FIREMEN

The earliest known photograph of the Wokingham Volunteer Fire Brigade, with the hand pump, 1870s.

The fire engine team being led across the Market Place to the fire station from their stables at the Rose Inn, *c.* 1912.

Here the engine is on call at the Waterloo Hotel, Crowthorne, *c.* 1912.

As early as 1625 it was decreed that there should be provision made in the Town Hall or some convenient place to deal with any fires in the town, in the form of twenty-five good leather buckets, three long ladders and two or more 'sufficient great iron hooks'. All the burgesses had to provide two buckets and an eighteen rung ladder at their homes. From 1887 the fire station was located in the new Town Hall; there was provision for the voluntary firemen and the engine, and the fire engines remained in the Town Hall until as recently as 1969. In this picture the 'Alert' steamer crew are off to deal with a fire in about 1900.

Here the crew is gathered in front of a local church, which seems to have been gutted before they could arrive, 1920s.

The engine was also used during the last war.

This was Mr Hawkins', the local undertaker's, pride and joy. The beautiful new self-contained machine dates from the early 1930s. It is being driven by Mr Trill.

Frederick Caiger's funeral after fifty years service with the Wokingham Fire Brigade, 1927.

SCHOOLS AND
CHURCHES

A group of children outside the Baptist Sunday School in Milton Road, c. 1910. The
building was originally a school and was founded in 1808.

Well-dressed children in the garden behind Montague House, when it was a private school.

The White House School in Finchampstead Road. Miss Caldwell used to live here when it became a preparatory school after the last war.

The field on which St Crispin's School was built in 1953 was called the Plantation. Annual air displays took place there in the 1930s, performed by the Sky Devil Air Circus. Flights were given, and many Wokingham people had their first trips there. During the war it was an emergency airfield, and at least one aeroplane is reported to have landed there. In the middle foreground can be seen the mark of the crater of a German aerial torpedo which fell there in the war.

County Council Schools, Wokingham.

Wescott Road Council School was built in 1905 for 396 children, to cater for the first extension to the town at the turn of the century. A further building was erected in 1911 for woodwork, cookery and the evening continuation classes. Many Wokingham children have been educated here over the past eighty or more years. It catered for boys and girls up to the school leaving age (fourteen or fifteen). The road was named to commemorate the town's first mayor, Thomas Manley Wescott.

Teaching was of the formal kind, as can be seen from the picture of a class in the 1920s. The classroom is the same today except for the desks, and there is now a false ceiling added. The school is now for infants only.

Some of the pupils, *c.* 1920.

The children were segregated at playtime – the boys to one side of the school and the girls to the other. Here the boys have been brought out to pose for the photographer.

Playtime in a cold winter in the 1920s: all the boys wore their caps in those days.

All Saints' Church, early 1860s. The twelfth-century Norman building, possibly on the site of an earlier Saxon church, was largely rebuilt in the fifteenth century.

The church, photographed from a different angle in London Road. It still looks very much the same today.

The particularly attractive Baptist church in Milton Road was erected on the site of an earlier building in 1860.

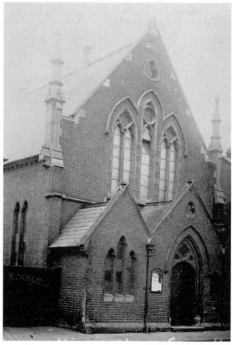

There was a Primitive Methodist church in Denmark Street, but the Wesleyans built theirs in Rose Street in 1870, on the site of the older Barn chapel.

The Wokingham Salvation Army Corps, 1915. Most of the band had gone off to fight in the War – but the big drum was still there! The Salvation Army came to Wokingham some time before 1888; it soon closed down, but was revived again in 1906. At that time the Hall was in Rose Street close to where Boots Opticians is today. It closed again in 1919 and re-opened in 1931, using the building previously occupied by the Primitive Methodists alongside the Red Cross clinic at the bottom of Denmark Street. They moved into Sturges Road just before the Second World War, the building up to that time having been used as a furniture depository, following its early use as a Gospel Hall. It was purchased by the Salvation Army in about 1942, at which time the officer there was one Captain Ernest Fiddaman, later to become a Church of England priest, and greatly loved as Father Fiddaman, the chaplain of the Royal British Legion in the town.

St Paul's church was built by John Walter of Bearwood in 1862 and enlarged in 1873.

Church House in Easthampstead Road was opened in 1902. During the First World War it was used by the Red Cross Voluntary Aid Detachment as an emergency hospital, and a plaque on the outside wall commemorates this. The turret was removed in 1964.

PUBS AND PLACES

The Pin and Bowl, a quiet little eighteenth-century pub, stood between the railway bridges

in Finchampstead Road; it was reduced to a pile of rubble for development in 1995. This

rural scene shows it and the bridge over the brook in 1922.

The Duke's Head, *c.* 1900. The building is much the same today apart from the position of the doors. It is at the bottom of Langborough Road.

The famous Rose Inn appears in many pictures, but few of them show the back. This one, dating from the 1950s, was taken before the spate of fires that have occurred there in recent years.

The Bush was a favourite hostelry. It is now shops but still retains its fine appearance. It is seen here in the 1950s.

The Dog and Duck at Emmbrook, 1930s.

The Olde Leathern Bottle in Barkham Road was much used by cyclists in the early days of the craze. It was photographed in the 1930s.

The Two Poplars, 1920s. The popular pub in Finchampstead Road still looks like this: the two poplars have been replaced by new ones and are doing well.

The Railway Hotel in the early 1920s, before becoming The Molly Millar. Recently it has been re-named again, most inappropriately, Big Hand Mo's Good Time Emporium, by an absentee landlord brewer.

The Redan in Peach Street, named after the famous Crimean War battle.

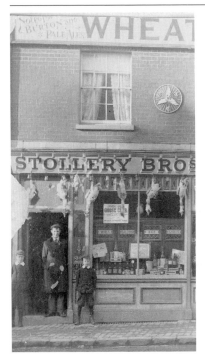

The middle portion of this picture is missing. It was the Wheatsheaf Inn in the Market Place, now occupied by Oddbins.

Another view of the Redan. The houses on the right were replaced by the Woolworth block in 1935.

Bearwood, the house built by John Walter of *The Times*, became the Royal Merchant Seaman's Orphanage. Today it is a private school, Bearwood College. During the First World War it was taken over as a Canadian convalescent hospital, temporary huts being built in the grounds at the rear.

Bearwood in all its Victorian splendour.

Still in the grounds of Bearwood, this picture shows two girls walking towards what was the converted old stables, during the First World War. These are now used as a junior house for the school.

Pinewood sanatorium was a convalescent home for wounded soldiers when this photograph was taken, in the First World War. It later became a TB hospital and is now a leisure centre.

The original house at Pinewood, during the First World War.

The fine police station with motorcycle squad, 1930s.

A most elegant building, the police station was designed by Morris, the Reading architect who was responsible for many houses in Murdoch and Sturges Road.

Buckhurst looks much like this today. William Heelas came to Wokingham in the 1780s, the family owned the draper's shop and farmed at Buckhurst, living in the Manor. Later Murdoch, the MP for Reading, lived there and in about 1928 it became a nursing home run by nuns. Now it is the Stakis St Anne's Manor Hotel and is in an excellent state of preservation.

The Workhouse or Union, now Wokingham Hospital, was built in 1850 to replace the old workhouse in Denmark Street.

Montague House, Broad Street, when it contained club rooms for HM Forces, 1915. It was built by Henry Montague in the 1690s, was a school in 1790, and Grosvenor school in 1928 after that establishment moved from Tudor House. It is now the library and adult education centre.

The garden at the back of Montague House, 1920s. This is soon to become a car park for the new town centre development.

Wixenford, a nineteenth-century house, photographed in the 1930s. It is now Ludgrove School.

Beches Manor became a hotel and burnt down in the late 1950s. In the grounds of the building now stands the new Youth and Community Centre in Reading Road, beside the Holt School.

The main building and ballroom at California in England near Arborfield. It was built in the 1930s and became a holiday camp.

This cut-down Austin Ten dragged the childrens' train around the Longmoor lake, close to the building shown above.

These lovely rest gardens were the gardens of St Paul's vicarage, which is now the District Council offices. Much of the garden is now car park, but some of the trees and the lake survive.

W.T. Martin, an alderman of the borough who lived in The Terrace, built an open-air swimming pool for the private use of his family. He sold it to the Borough in 1946 and it was a popular venue for Wokingham people. In 1992 it was sold as a building site to pay for the new Carnival Pool.

Acknowledgements

It would not have been possible to have written this book without the help of many friends, some of whom provided the illustrations and others either details of their families or their own reminiscences. My grateful thanks to Ken and Edna Goatley, without whom much about the history of the town would have been forgotten; they also provided many of the pictures. To Michael Curling for access to his vast collection of Wokingham postcards and photographs, and also to Brian Eighteen for allowing me to select items from his equally good collection.

In particular, I am indebted to Mr F. Caiger, Marion Ogden (née Perkins), Mr Cecil Culver, Mrs Jefferies, Mr May, Mrs Helen Headington, Miss Mary Cole, Mr Stan Harris, Mrs Stevens, Celia Read, Monica Parsons and Bert May of the *Wokingham Times* for some of the pictures from their files, and to Carol Carson of Wokingham Public Library for the use of pictures in their charge.

Every effort has been made to establish copyright and permission has been obtained to reproduce pictures where required, but if any copyright photograph has been used inadvertently sincere apologies are tended.

BRITAIN IN OLD PHOTOGRAPHS

To order any of these titles please telephone Littlehampton Book Services on 01903 721596

ALDERNEY

Alderney: A Second Selection, *B Bonnard*

BEDFORDSHIRE

Bedfordshire at Work, *N Lutt*

BERKSHIRE

Maidenhead, *M Hayles & D Hedges*
Around Maidenhead, *M Hayles & B Hedges*
Reading, *P Southerton*
Reading: A Second Selection, *P Southerton*
Sandhurst and Crowthorne, *K Dancy*
Around Slough, *J Hunter & K Hunter*
Around Thatcham, *P Allen*
Around Windsor, *B Hedges*

BUCKINGHAMSHIRE

Buckingham and District, *R Cook*
High Wycombe, *R Goodearl*
Around Stony Stratford, *A Lambert*

CHESHIRE

Cheshire Railways, *M Hitches*
Chester, *S Nichols*

CLWYD

Clwyd Railways, *M Hitches*

CLYDESDALE

Clydesdale, *Lesmahagow Parish Historical Association*

CORNWALL

Cornish Coast, *T Bowden*
Falmouth, *P Gilson*
Lower Fal, *P Gilson*
Around Padstow, *M McCarthy*
Around Penzance, *J Holmes*
Penzance and Newlyn, *J Holmes*
Around Truro, *A Lyne*
Upper Fal, *P Gilson*

CUMBERLAND

Cockermouth and District, *J Bernard Bradbury*
Keswick and the Central Lakes, *J Marsh*
Around Penrith, *F Boyd*
Around Whitehaven, *H Fancy*

DERBYSHIRE

Derby, *D Buxton*
Around Matlock, *D Barton*

DEVON

Colyton and Seaton, *T Gosling*
Dawlish and Teignmouth, *G Gosling*
Devon Aerodromes, *K Saunders*
Exeter, *P Thomas*
Exmouth and Budleigh Salterton, *T Gosling*
From Haldon to Mid-Dartmoor, *T Hall*
Honiton and the Otter Valley, *J Yallop*
Around Kingsbridge, *K Tanner*
Around Seaton and Sidmouth, *T Gosling*
Seaton, Axminster and Lyme Regis, *T Gosling*

DORSET

Around Blandford Forum, *B Cox*
Bournemouth, *M Colman*
Bridport and the Bride Valley, *J Burrell & S Humphries*
Dorchester, *T Gosling*
Around Gillingham, *P Crocker*

DURHAM

Darlington, *G Flynn*
Darlington: A Second Selection, *G Flynn*
Durham People, *M Richardson*
Houghton-le-Spring and Hetton-le-Hole, *K Richardson*
Houghton-le-Spring and Hetton-le-Hole:
  A Second Selection, *K Richardson*
Sunderland, *S Miller & B Bell*
Teesdale, *D Coggins*
Teesdale: A Second Selection, *P Raine*
Weardale, *J Crosby*
Weardale: A Second Selection, *J Crosby*

DYFED

Aberystwyth and North Ceredigion,
  Dyfed Cultural Services Dept
Haverfordwest, *Dyfed Cultural Services Dept*
Upper Tywi Valley, *Dyfed Cultural Services Dept*

ESSEX

Around Grays, *B Evans*

GLOUCESTERSHIRE

Along the Avon from Stratford to Tewkesbury, *J Jeremiah*
Cheltenham: A Second Selection, *R Whiting*
Cheltenham at War, *P Gill*
Cirencester, *J Welsford*
Around Cirencester, *E Cuss & P Griffiths*
Forest, The, *D Mullin*
Gloucester, *J Voyce*
Around Gloucester, *A Sutton*
Gloucester: From the Walwin Collection, *J Voyce*
North Cotswolds, *D Viner*
Severn Vale, *A Sutton*
Stonehouse to Painswick, *A Sutton*
Stroud and the Five Valleys, *S Gardiner & L Padin*
Stroud and the Five Valleys: A Second Selection,
  S Gardiner & L Padin
Stroud's Golden Valley, *S Gardiner & L Padin*
Stroudwater and Thames & Severn Canals,
  E Cuss & S Gardiner
Stroudwater and Thames & Severn Canals: A Second
  Selection, *E Cuss & S Gardiner*
Tewkesbury and the Vale of Gloucester, *C Hilton*
Thornbury to Berkeley, *J Hudson*
Uley, Dursley and Cam, *A Sutton*
Wotton-under-Edge to Chipping Sodbury, *A Sutton*

GWYNEDD

Anglesey, *M Hitches*
Gwynedd Railways, *M Hitches*
Around Llandudno, *M Hitches*
Vale of Conwy, *M Hitches*

HAMPSHIRE

Gosport, *J Sadden*
Portsmouth, *P Rogers & D Francis*

HEREFORDSHIRE

Herefordshire, *A Sandford*

HERTFORDSHIRE

Barnet, *I Norrie*
Hitchin, *A Fleck*
St Albans, *S Mullins*
Stevenage, *M Appleton*

ISLE OF MAN

The Tourist Trophy, *B Snelling*

ISLE OF WIGHT

Newport, *D Parr*
Around Ryde, *D Parr*

JERSEY

Jersey: A Third Selection, *R Lemprière*

KENT

Bexley, *M Scott*
Broadstairs and St Peter's, *J Whyman*
Bromley, Keston and Hayes, *M Scott*
Canterbury: A Second Selection, *D Butler*
Chatham and Gillingham, *P MacDougall*
Chatham Dockyard, *P MacDougall*
Deal, *J Broady*
Early Broadstairs and St Peter's, *B Wootton*
East Kent at War, *D Collyer*
Eltham, *J Kennett*
Folkestone: A Second Selection, *A Taylor & E Rooney*
Goudhurst to Tenterden, *A Guilmant*
Gravesend, *R Hiscock*
Around Gravesham, *R Hiscock & D Grierson*
Herne Bay, *J Hawkins*
Lympne Airport, *D Collyer*
Maidstone, *I Hales*
Margate, *R Clements*
RAF Hawkinge, *R Humphreys*
RAF Manston, *RAF Manston History Club*
RAF Manston: A Second Selection,
  RAF Manston History Club
Ramsgate and Thanet Life, *D Perkins*
Romney Marsh, *E Carpenter*
Sandwich, *C Wanostrocht*
Around Tonbridge, *C Bell*
Tunbridge Wells, *M Rowlands & I Beavis*
Tunbridge Wells: A Second Selection,
  M Rowlands & I Beavis
Around Whitstable, *C Court*
Wingham, Adisham and Littlebourne, *M Crane*

LANCASHIRE

Around Barrow-in-Furness, *J Garbutt & J Marsh*
Blackpool, *C Rothwell*
Bury, *J Hudson*
Chorley and District, *J Smith*
Fleetwood, *C Rothwell*
Heywood, *J Hudson*
Around Kirkham, *C Rothwell*
Lancashire North of the Sands, *J Garbutt & J Marsh*
Around Lancaster, *S Ashworth*
Lytham St Anne's, *C Rothwell*
North Fylde, *C Rothwell*
Radcliffe, *J Hudson*
Rossendale, *B Moore & N Dunnachie*

LEICESTERSHIRE

Around Ashby-de-la-Zouch, *K Hillier*
Charnwood Forest, *I Keil, W Humphrey & D Wix*
Leicester, *D Burton*
Leicester: A Second Selection, *D Burton*
Melton Mowbray, *T Hickman*
Around Melton Mowbray, *T Hickman*
River Soar, *D Wix, P Shacklock & I Keil*
Rutland, *T Clough*
Vale of Belvoir, *T Hickman*
Around the Welland Valley, *S Mastoris*

LINCOLNSHIRE

Grimsby, *J Tierney*
Around Grimsby, *J Tierney*
Grimsby Docks, *J Tierney*
Lincoln, *D Cuppleditch*